F IN

EXAMS

Back again with MORE of the funniest exam-paper blunders

Richard Benson

summersdale

Contents

Introduction

Some people just aren't cut out for exams. They'll put down a best guess that's so wrong it's almost right, or maybe they'll just get downright ridiculous. Luckily, *F in Exams* is here to gather up these hugely inaccurate and unconventional answers in another fine selection for your amusement. Whatever the subject, these wild stabs, misfires and own goals will have you sympathising, sniggering and thanking the exam gods it's not you in the hot seat.

Subject: **Biology**

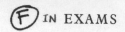

Name the life process of getting rid of waste.

Bin day

Athlete's foot is an infection of the feet caused by what?

Too much athletics.

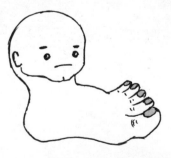

Biology

Describe two effects on women's health during menstruation.

What does it have to do with men? I think it should really be called womenstruation.

What did Charles Darwin mean by the term 'natural selection'?

When you go to a garden centre to pick out some nice plants.

Referring to the diagram above, name the type of organism that is at the top of a pyramid of biomass.

Hedwig.

Biology

Describe one common symptom of a fever.

Not wanting to go to school

What is the process by which the skin loses water?

Crying

Some people hold the view that elderly people should not be allowed to drive.
Give one way in which old age can affect someone's ability to drive.

Walking sticks get in the way of the steering wheel.

Eating a balanced diet is very important in order to maintain a healthy body.
What does a 'balanced' diet mean?

One quarter burger, three quarters chips.

The photograph above shows a male sheep. Offer an explanation for two of its physical characteristics.

It has curly head tubes to help it hear better.
It has got legs so it's not confused with a cloud.

13

Biogas is a biofuel. What is the main gas that makes up biogas?

Bio.

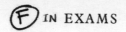

During intense exercise, a person's body heat increases. Explain how the brain controls body temperature.

It makes you want to give up and lie down to cool off.

Subject: **Chemistry**

Science sucks

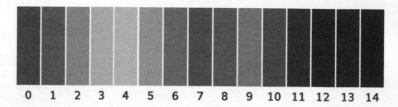

The diagram above shows the pH scale. Complete the following sentence:

Number 7 on the pH scale means that the solution is

Grimy .

Thermometers are used to measure temperature. When a log fire is alight, what happens to objects around the fire?

If they're marshmallows, they get crispy on the outside and gooey on the inside.

16

Complete the following equation:
Acid + metal oxide → ____.

A science experiment waiting to happen

Carbon has many different forms. One of these is diamond. Give two properties of diamond.

Being forever.
Being a girl's best friend.

The symbol above might be found in a laboratory. What does it mean?

May set hair alight

Give one use for the periodic table.

It tells you what lessons you have and when.

The Earth's atmosphere is composed of several gases. Name two.

Farts and clouds.

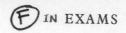

A mole is a term used by chemists all over the world. Explain what this terms refers to.

A small, furry, burrowing creature.

Why is it important that you wear goggles when conducting an experiment?

So you feel like a real scientist.

Figure 1

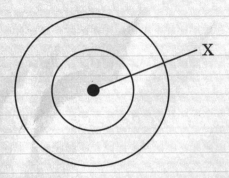

Figure 1 shows a diagram of an atom. What does X represent in the diagram?

Bullseye.

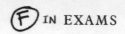

Alloys are useful in the manufacture of many products. What is an alloy?

A friend who has your back.

You can soften hard water. Name the substance that can be used to soften hard water.

Water softener

Subject: **Physics**

WIZARD
OF
KNOWLEDGE

Electricity is transferred from power stations to consumers through the National Grid. Name a reason why a house located in the highlands or in a mountainous area would not be connected to the National Grid.

Everything is goat-powered.

What is meant by the term 'radioactivity'?

Exercising to music.

Figure 2

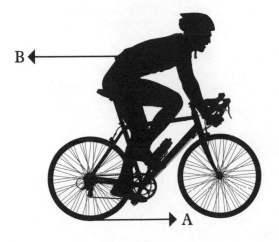

The diagram above shows a cyclist with an arrow underneath, labelled A.

Forces are acting on the person and the bicycle. What is the cause of the force labelled A?

They've hit a hedgehog.

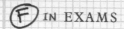 IN EXAMS

In the box below, draw a diagram of a working electric circuit, including four different components.

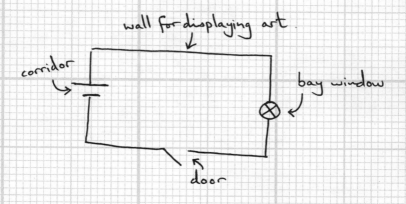

wall for displaying art.

corridor

bay window

door

Name a feature of a dwarf planet, such as Pluto.

SMALL AND HAS A LARGE BEARD, AND SOMETIMES CARRIES AN AXE.

Atoms can be represented by the symbol: $^A_Z X$
What is 'A' in this symbol?

The first letter of the alphabet

The model of the atom evolved over time as physicists conducted further study.

In the space below, draw the 'plum pudding' model of the atom and label it where necessary.

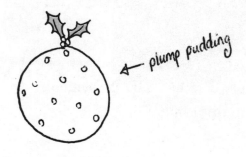

← plump pudding

Cameras are designed to capture an image seen by the eye, and represent this image in high definition. Describe one thing that the eye and a camera have in common.

They're round, mostly.

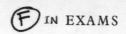

When an X-ray is taken, the radiographer who is taking the X-ray has to either leave the room or stand behind a screen. Explain why the radiographer must do this.

So they can't see your rude bits.

Ultrasound has many different uses. What is meant by the term 'ultrasound'?

Sound that's so loud, it's more than sound.

Subject: ......**DraMa**.........................

WOW!

ooooOh
La La

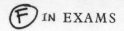

Explain what a 'framing device' is.

It's usually made of glass and wood and you can put pictures in it to hang on a wall.

What role does an 'understudy' play in theatre productions?

To act out the play at the same time as the main cast, but in the study that's underneath the stage.

Drama

Describe a time you have experienced effective use of sound during a live theatre production.

When the orchestra played loudly to drown out bad singing.

Think about Shakespeare's *A Midsummer Night's Dream*. Explain how the role of Bottom enhanced the play.

Without Bottom, the actors would've had nothing to sit on and their trousers would've fallen down.

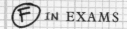
Sketch a costume idea for one of the characters in *An Ideal Husband* by Oscar Wilde.

AN IDEAL HUSBAND

Treats me
like a
princess

Does all the
cooking

Give an example of how cues might be used in a dramatic performance.

For any scenes featuring snooker or pool.

Name the distinctive feature of a theatre 'in the round'.

The actors all say the same lines but one starts a bit after the first, then another, then another, etc.

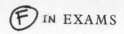

Describe a theme that runs throughout the musical theatre production *Les Misérables*.

It's miserable being French.

Consider *Macbeth* by William Shakespeare. Give an example of foreshadowing in the play.

The brims on the witches hats mean their foreheads are in the shadows.

Drama

Give details of your idea for a set design for a performance of *The 39 Steps*.

A very large staircase.

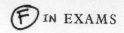

What is a 'prop'?

The person who props up the hooker in a rugby scrum.

In Greek tragedy, what is the typical role of the chorus?

It's the part where you get to sing along.

Subject: *English Language and Literature*

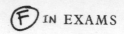

In one scene featured in *Romeo and Juliet*, the nurse calls Juliet 'Ladybird' and 'Lamb'. What do these terms tell you about the nurse's thoughts towards Juliet?

She has trouble remembering Juliet's name.

Explain, in your own words, the impact that Shakespeare had on modern language.

Not much. Nobody says 'forsooth' or 'thou' any more

How does the title of the novel *The Curious Incident of the Dog in the Night-Time* relate to the plot?

It's a curious story, there's a dog in it and it takes place at night.

Explain what is meant by the word 'hyperbole'.

Better than the Superbole.

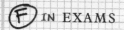

The following extract is from the poem 'To His Coy Mistress' by Andrew Marvell.

My vegetable love should grow
Vaster than empires and more slow;
An hundred years should go to praise
Thine eyes, and on thy forehead gaze;

What do you think the poet is trying to convey in this extract?

She's got something on her forehead that keeps distracting him (maybe a vegetable?)

Imagine that you are trying to help more schoolchildren take up a sport. Name the sport you have chosen and write a persuasive statement in order to encourage others to get involved.

Computer gaming — you can sit down, eat crisps while you play and you can't get injured.

What term can be used to describe the following statement: 'Life is a rollercoaster.'

A song (by Ronan Keating)

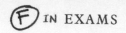

Use the word 'accost' in a sentence.

We fancied a coffee so
we went to accost-a.

Describe a time when you once lied or cheated. You will be assessed on the quality of your language, spelling, grammar and punctuation.

I cheated on this exam by
smuggling in some notes.

Suggest one way that newspapers could use text and font to appeal more to readers.

Use text and font to write 'FREE CAKE WITH EVERY NEWSPAPER' on the front page.

SNAIL
SNAIL
SNAIL

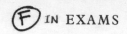 IN EXAMS

List three different types of poetry in the space below.

Vases, mugs and bowls.

What is a 'syllable'?

A TYPE OF FISH.

Subject: Geography

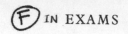

Explain one benefit of the growth of science parks in the UK.

fresh air for all
the local nerds

Define 'food security' and suggest one way in which it can be improved.

Writing your name on things
in the fridge – you could use
stickers to make it clearer.

What is meant by 'fracking'?

It's a naughty word, like frigging.

How do we measure wind speed?

By how fast someone
else smells it

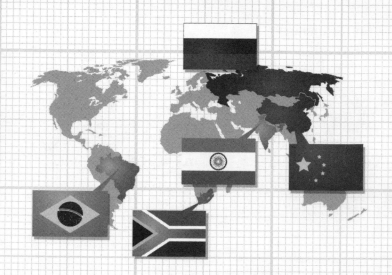

The image above shows the five BRICS countries.
Explain what they all have in common.

They all produce large amounts
of bricks.

Geography

Describe one negative effect of 'traffic congestion' and suggest a way in which traffic congestion can be reduced.

You get a bunged-up nose and throat from all the fumes — you could use a menthol vapour rub to help clear your sinuses.

Name one push factor and one pull factor that causes people to move from rural areas to cities.

PUSH : tractors behind you
PULL : tractors in front of you

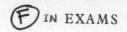

Some people believe that the weather in the UK is becoming increasingly extreme. In your own words, explain why this could be the case.

Brexit.

In an urban context, what do the letters in the abbreviation 'CBD' stand for?

Curly Brown Dogpoo

Geography

There are multiple ways that flooding can be managed. Flood management can be separated into hard and soft engineering techniques. What is meant by 'hard' and 'soft' in this context?

Hard means really tricky to do, like buying everyone a boat.

Soft means easy, like giving free hugs to those who've had their homes ruined.

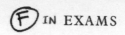

Use the term 'delta' in a sentence to demonstrate your knowledge of the term.

Delta force are a group of special forces soldiers from America.

Give one reason why an increasing 'ageing population' could be a problem with regard to a society's resources.

The post office will be packed.

Subject:  **History**

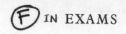

One of Winston Churchill's famous speeches included the phrase 'we shall fight on the beaches'. What did he mean by this?

The Nazis would not stop us from enjoying seaside holidays.

Explain what happened during the 'Bay of Pigs' incident in 1961.

A bay was filled with loads of pigs - there were just too many pigs.

How did the Wars of the Roses impact England in the fifteenth century?

People struggled to get hold of fresh flowers.

Describe what is meant by the term 'capitalism'.

Using a big letter at the start of sentences.

Why does the flag shown above feature thirteen stars rather than fifty?

It was probably hometime so the flagmaker didn't finish it.

What is the name of the movement that successfully gained women the right to vote?

Sufferingism

Martin Luther King Jr was famous for his 'I Have a Dream' speech. In your own words, explain what he meant by this phrase.

I had a nap and saw things while my eyes were closed.

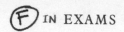

Consumer goods	1920	1929
Cars	9 million	26 million
Radios	60 thousand	10 million
Telephones	13 million	20 million

The figures above show the production of consumer goods in America throughout the 1920s. What do these figures tell you about American society during this period?

1921-1928 were erased from history.

Julius Caesar was a Roman general and politician in the first century BCE.

Take a look at the photograph above showing a statue of him. What impressions do you get about Julius Caesar from this depiction?

He could play a mean air guitar.

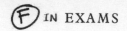
What did Elizabeth I mean when she said in a speech, 'I know I have the body of a weak, feeble woman, but I have the heart and stomach of a king'?

She had bits of Henry VIII stored in her freezer.

Explain the significance of the Boston tea party (1773) for American independence.

It made them realise they were perfectly capable of throwing a great party without the help of the English.

yum!

Subject: **HOME ECONOMICS**

When making meringue, it is common to add vinegar. Explain why.

Vinegar goes well with chips, which are crispy on the outside, softer on the inside – just like meringues.

Give the term used to describe bacteria found in frozen foods.

Ice bugs.

Explain why it is so important to reheat food to the correct temperature.

If it's too cold, it's disgusting.
If it's too hot, it burns your mouth.

Name one common element in foods such as cakes and pastries that make them more attractive than healthier foods such as cucumbers and cabbages.

Fancy icing.

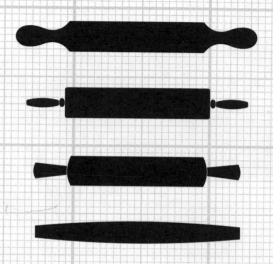

Suggest three ways the above utensils might be used.

1. A BRACELET HOLDER
2. PERCUSSION
3. CUT THEM OUT AND USE THEM AS PAPER MOUSTACHES.

Name an example of a protein and provide an advantage of including this particular protein in your diet.

Burgers. The advantage of burgers is that you don't have to cook them yourself – you can just buy them from McDonalds or Burger King.

Give one method of preserving meat.

Lock it up in a cupboard so no one can eat it.

Samantha is doing a marathon on Saturday. In the space below sketch a potential main meal Samantha could have on Friday night which would give her energy for the marathon. Label the meal to explain why you think each component would be beneficial.

Runner beans, for running.

In the space below, sketch an idea of suitable packaging for a new food product. The product must be a sweet type of food aimed at young people aged 16–20. Consider the different factors required to make your packaging appeal to its target audience.

SUGAR

VERSATILE

What is meant by the term 'shelf life'?

The amount of time a shelf is likely to last before it falls down.

More people are turning towards a vegan diet. Define the term 'veganism' and provide an example of a main meal that would be suitable for a vegan.

Veganism is being a fussy eater. A main meal would be just rice, with a side of rice.

Subject: ....**ICT**.........

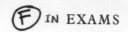

Describe one way in which using Powerpoint can help enhance a presentation.

You couldn't even do a presentation without a power point - how would you plug anything in?

What is an 'input device'?

A fork or a spoon.

When new software is created, it is protected by copyright laws. Explain what is meant by 'copyright.'

You have a right to copy the software and share it with your friends.

In a sentence, say why you agree or disagree with the following claim: 'robots would be better workers than humans.'

You don't have to make them tea or pretend to like them.

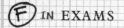

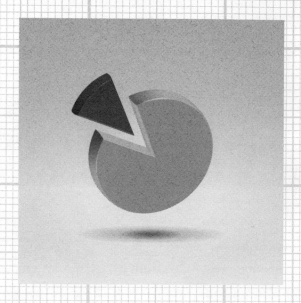

Data can be visually represented in many forms. The image above shows an example of what?

Pacman eating a slice of pizza

Teleworking has seen the relocation of businesses and the rise of people working from home.
Name two advantages of teleworking.

No one can tell if you're working, because they can't see you.

Explain two ways in which the rise of IT can be detrimental to human health.

The popularity of the film led to a rise in killer clowns.

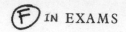

Name one reason why it is useful to purchase a microphone with a desktop computer.

You might need it at Same point.

Give an example of a secure password between 8 and 10 characters in length.

9charactersinlength

New careers have arisen from the rise in ICT, especially via social media websites such as YouTube and Instagram. Describe one way in which money can be generated from the use of social media.

You can take other peoples' data and sell it to other companies.

WHAT.

77

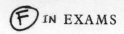

What are cookies?

Delicias biscuits with chocolate chips.

Define what is meant by a 'dongle'.

A penis

Subject: **Maths**

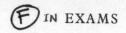
What are 'surds'?

The bubbles that come from soap.

Work out what the pattern is in the following sequence.
1, 5, 9, 13, 17

The numbers get bigger.

Maths

Describe what an irrational number is.

Numbers that don't make any sense, like twelvety-zero.

Angela sees a dress she wants in a '20% off' sale. The original price of the garment was £40. What is the price of the dress after the discount has been applied?

20% percent less than before.

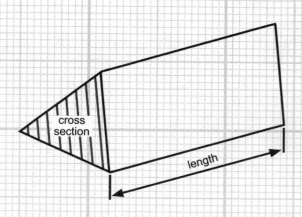

cross section

length

The diagram above shows a prism. The area of the cross-section of the prism is 4 cm² and the length of the prism is 6 cm. What is the volume of the prism?

It is silent, unless you hit it with something.

Maths

A plane leaves London at 10.24 and takes 2 hours 15 minutes to get to Barcelona. Barcelona is 1 hour ahead of the UK. What time would it be when the plane lands in Barcelona?

A different time to the time in the UK.

In a cafe, Lucy buys two cups of tea, amounting to £3.50. Gilly buys four cups of tea and three cups of coffee. Her total comes to £14.50. How much is the price of one cup of coffee?

Free if Gilly has enough points on her loyalty card.

In the space below, draw a factor tree of the number 54.

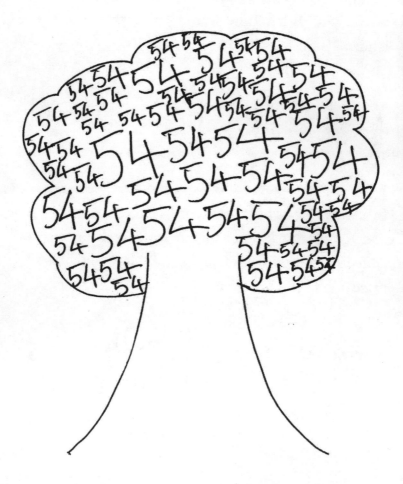

What is a 'trapezium'?

A room for keeping trapeze artists in.

Draw a quadrilateral in the space below.

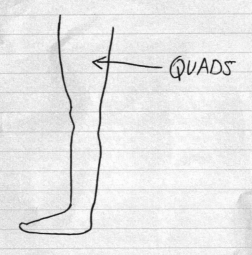

QUADS

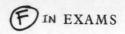

David is asked to flip a coin 100 times. Before he begins, he is asked to give the probability of the coin landing on heads on the hundredth flip. What should David say?

'Heads or tails?'

Provide an example of a rational fraction.

When something is only a little bit rational.

Subject: .....**Music**...

What is a 'hoe-down'?

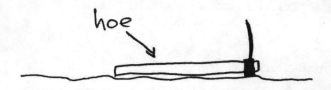

Give one example of a membranophone.

I think he owns one
of the football clubs?

Define the term 'time signature'.

How fast you can sign your name.

What is meant by the term 'Baroque'?

He used to be the President of America.

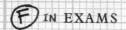
Label the keys of this section of a piano keyboard.

KEYS

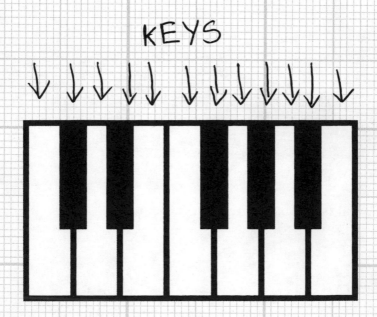

Music

Music has evolved and taken on many different forms as a result of the rise in ICT. Name a genre of music that has become more popular since the rise of ICT.

Illegally downloaded music.

Describe what is meant by the term 'calypso'.

A fruit-flavoured ice lolly.

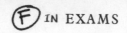

Explain what 'sympathic vibration' means.

When one person can tell what another person is thinking just by looking at them.

What is meant by the term 'horn stab' in a musical context?

It's when a bull gets mad after hearing flamenco music and it attacks a matador.

Music

What is a major characteristic of the genre of music
known as 'reggae'?

Dreadlocks.

Provide two reasons why the Beatles decided to stop
touring by 1966.

Their bus broke down.

They ran out of shoes.

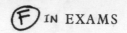

Do you think a band's name can influence their popularity? Explain the reason(s) for your answer.

Not really. Nickelback is an awful name but they seem to have done OK.

Nowadays, most music producers make use of a DAW. What does DAW stand for?

Deep and windy.

Subject: .... **PE** ....

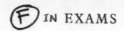

Spell out each of the words that comprise the acronym RICE with regard to sports injuries:

Random Injury - Can't Explain

In what ways can age affect an individual's participation in sport?

When you're older you fall asleep more, which is not good if you're in the middle of a game.

Give two reasons why the consumption of alcohol can have negative effects on athletes in training.

They can't run in a straight line after a drink.

Jesse Owens participated in the 1936 Berlin Olympics. Name one of his achievements there.

He managed to get out of Germany alive.

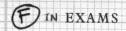

The diagrams below show two different types of contraction.

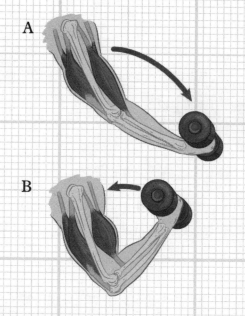

A

B

Label A and B, describing these muscle contractions.

A: the arm is going
   downwards.

B: the arm is going
   upwards.

In what ways can youth sports be funded? Make two suggestions other than through charitable donations.

Find some buried treasure.
Bake sales.

In your own words, explain why 'gym culture' has seen a sharp increase in recent years.

To post fitness photos on Instagram.

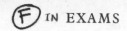

Suggest a method that can be used to assess an individual's physical fitness during PE in schools.

Make them run and time how long it takes them to collapse.

Name one way of training that can help to improve one's strength.

Arm wrestling.

The image above shows a weightlifter in training. Describe two qualities, mental or physical, required to perform the action pictured.

- Being bald
- Big veins

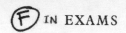

Name two immediate effects of intense exercise.

Not wanting to do any more exercise.
Body odour.

Define the term 'tidal volume'.

When you're by the sea and the
waves are crashing really loud.

Subject: **Religious Studies**

YAY!

Which tradition is the above symbol associated with?

PIRATES!

What is a kippah?

A stinky ~~fish~~ fish
my dad likes to eat.

Religious Studies

What does the term 'nirvana' refer to?

Really loud, depressing music from the 90s.

What does the symbol shown above tell us about the ancient Chinese and their beliefs?

They like tadpoles.

In Hinduism, the god Vishnu is believed to have a number of avatars. What is an avatar?

It's a blue alien with white speckles on its face and pointy ears.

List two types of evil.

Maths and English.

Explain what the term 'divine creation' means.

It's a big compliment.

What is the significance of Easter Sunday?

Delicious chocolate eggs.

The image above shows a Christian marriage ceremony taking place. Why is marriage so important to Christians?

It gets all the non-Christians to actually go to cherch.

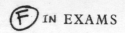

The image above shows Jesus. What conclusions can you draw from this depiction?

He liked lambs.

Subject: **Technology + Design**

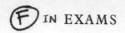

A triangular symbol featuring a lion's head can often be found on packaging for children's toys. What does the symbol mean?

Not suitable for lions.

What is meant by the term 'smart materials'?

Books and study guides that increase your brainpower.

Why should you always carry out a risk assessment before using equipment such as a sewing machine?

You might sew your hand to your face and then you have a hand sewn to your face.

Give a definition of the term 'consumerism'.

eating loads.

The image above is of a template for a promotional brochure. In what ways could you change the design of this brochure to make it look more appealing? If it helps, you can sketch your ideas in the space below.

IT LOOKS BORING. ADD MORE DINOSAURS ON SKATEBOARDS + EXPLOSIONS.

Define the term 'target audience'.

The people standing at
an archery competition.

What is meant by the term 'intellectual property'?

A clever house.

Colour is an important component of product design. Using your own knowledge, give one example of the use of colour in a product and say why it is effective.

Blood is red, which is useful because it shows up well when you cut yourself.

Identify two things that a company must take into consideration when designing a new handheld games console.

• Where will the crumbs get stuck?

• Can it be used by someone with really chunky fingers?

The image above is for an item of food packaging. Describe one feature of this packaging and why it serves a useful purpose.

The box has no markings on the outside, so no one can see you and judge you for buying a big fat burger.

Subject: Business Studies and Economics

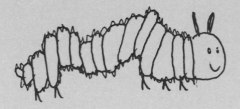

Greenpeace is an example of a pressure group which has launched campaigns against various industries and businesses. How might a Greenpeace campaign affect the reputation of a business?

They'll make people think that your shop kills whales when that might not be the case.

Often retailers such as coffee shops offer loyalty cards or reward schemes. Name one disadvantage of such schemes.

You have to buy about a hundred coffees before you get one free.

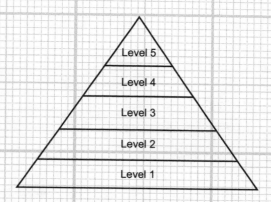

Businesses cater to human needs. The diagram above shows Maslow's hierarchy of needs. Draw one conclusion from the diagram.

Maslow had been to Egypt recently.

Name one benefit of being a 'sole trader'.

People always need shoes.

How can 'focus groups' be useful when businesses are thinking of creating a new product?

They're useful if you are making glasses.

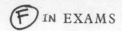

Define the term 'fringe benefit' in a business context.

It's good for hiding a big forehead.

What is the purpose of a 'forecast income statement'?

So you know if a storm is on its way.

The image above shows a container ship, used for transporting goods and raw materials across large distances. Give two disadvantages for a company that relies on the use of container ships.

Seasickness and bad food.

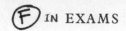

What does it mean to say that someone is 'underemployed'?

They work in the basement.

Ben is applying for an unpaid internship at a technology company based in Wales. Give one important factor that Ben should take into consideration when making his application.

Reconsider — you don't get paid.

The picture above shows a landfill site, where waste materials that cannot be recycled are dumped. How might a business justify its use of non-recyclable packaging?

At the landfill, the packaging with food left on it is a nice snack for seagulls.

Image Credits

F IN EXAMS

The Big Book of
Test Paper Blunders

Richard Benson

£9.99

Hardback

ISBN:978-1-84953-924-1

Exams have never been so hilarious!

Banish the horror of school days with this bumper edition of the world's ~~worst~~ best test paper blunders. Bursting with misunderstandings, misspellings and spirited – if ultimately incorrect – answers, this collection brings together the most head-scratching, side-splitting examples from the *F in Exams* series.

If you're interested in finding out more about our books, find us on Facebook at **Summersdale Publishers** and follow us on Twitter at @**Summersdale**.

www.summersdale.com